ENGLISH

Gillian Howell
Updated by Madeleine Barnes
Series Editor: **Richard Cooper**

RISING STARS

Rising Stars UK Ltd, 7 Hatchers Mews, Bermondsey Street, London SE1 3GS

www.risingstars-uk.com

All facts are correct at time of going to press.

First published 2003
Second edition 2008
Third edition 2010
This edition incorporating revisions 2014

Text, design and layout © Rising Stars UK Ltd 2014

First edition written by: Gill Matthews, Alison Clarke, Laura Collins and Richard Cooper
Second edition written by: Gillian Howell
Third edition updated by: Madeleine Barnes
Educational consultant: Lorna Pepper
Fourth edition educational consultant: Maria Richards
Project management and editorial: Bruce Nicholson
Illustrations: Phill Burrows, Clive Wakfer and Julian Baker
Design: Clive Sutherland
Cover design: Burville-Riley Partnership

Acknowledgements
p50 Photos iStock; p50 Reproduced with kind permission of Go Ape!, www.goape.co.uk; p52 Extract from the video interview with Valerie Bloom recorded for The Poetry Archive website at www.poetryarchive.org, reprinted by permission of Valerie Bloom and the Poetry Archive; p52 Reproduced with kind permission from *Bootleg* by Alex Shearer (Macmillan Children's Books, London, UK, 2003); p56 Reproduced with kind permission of The Society of Authors as the Literary Representative of the Estate of Alfred Noyes

Every effort has been made to trace copyright holders and obtain their permission for the use of copyright material. The authors and publishers will gladly receive information enabling them to rectify any error or omission in subsequent editions.

British Library Cataloguing in Publication Data
A CIP record for this book is available from the British Library.

ISBN 978-1-78339-415-9

Printed by Craft Print International Ltd., Singapore

Contents

How to use this book

Writing non-fiction

(1) **Definition** – This describes the genre and provides examples of the text type.

(2) **Text type** – Each type of writing is explained in a step-by-step way to help you plan.

(3) **Self-assessment** – Tick the face that best describes your understanding of this concept.

(4) **Text plan** – Planning is very important when writing fiction and non-fiction, and these charts will help you to plan properly.

(5) **Language features** – This explains the language features used for this type of text, including examples.

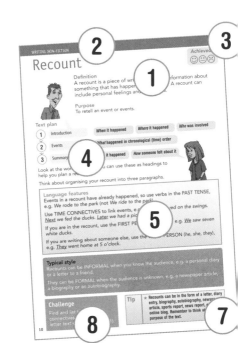

(6) **Text example** – This gives you an example of a well-written piece of text that follows the text plan and contains key language features.

(7) **Tips** – Here you are given key hints and tips to help you achieve Level 4.

(8) **Challenge** – Here you are asked to find features contained in the text example. The answers can be found on pages 61–63.

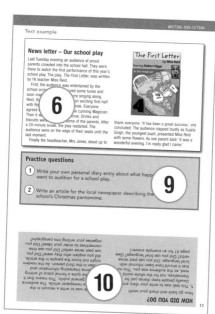

(9) **Practice questions** – This is where you do the work! Try answering the questions by using the text plan and by referring to the key language features. Compare your work with the written example – is it good enough for Level 4?

(10) **How did you do?** – Read the questions – can you answer 'yes' to each of them?

Writing fiction

This section takes you through the key elements of writing fiction:

(1) **Structure** – This section provides a model structure for your fiction writing including examples.

(2) **Setting, character and theme** – This section explains the key ingredients for writing fiction and explores each ingredient in depth.

(3) **Planning** – This section provides you with a structure to use before you begin writing a story.

(4) **Challenge** – The challenges ask you to find features contained in the text example.

(5) **Tips** – The tips give you ideas and hints to improve your work.

Reading comprehension

(1) **Text examples** – These give you typical examples of a piece of text that you might find in your National Tests.

(2) **Tips** – These give you suggestions on how to read the text and questions to ask yourself while reading.

(3) **Questions** – The text is followed by a number of questions relating to the text. There are 1-, 2- and 3-mark questions, so remember to read between the lines.

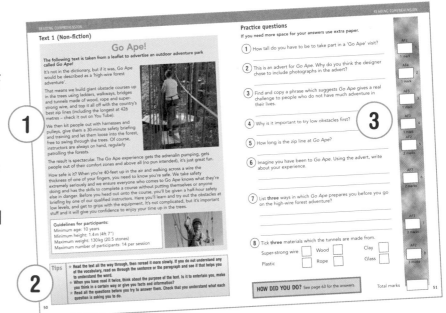

In addition you will find over 100 clear tips and facts to help you with: *grammar* *spelling* *punctuation* *vocabulary* *handwriting*

A glossary of terms can be found on page 59.

If you use this guidance to help you prepare for your test you will have a great chance of achieving Level 4!

About the National Tests

Key facts

- ★ The Key Stage 2 National Tests take place in the summer term in Year 6. You will be tested on Maths and English.

- ★ The tests take place in your school and will be marked by examiners – not your teacher!

- ★ Individual scores are not made public. However, a school's combined scores are published in what are commonly known as 'league tables'.

The National Tests for English

You will take three tests in English. These are designed to test your reading comprehension, grammar, punctuation and spelling. Your writing is now teacher assessed, along with handwriting.

The Reading Test

This is one test to assess your reading comprehension. In this test you will be given a series of texts and an answer booklet. You will have one hour to read the texts and complete the answer booklet section of the test. You use the texts to answer the questions so you do not need to memorise them. You should refer to the texts closely while you are answering. Some of the questions guide you to a particular page, 'Look at page 6,' but you will need to identify the correct text in other questions.

The Grammar, Punctuation and Spelling Test

The grammar and punctuation part of the test lasts 45 minutes. There are different types of questions for you to answer in different ways. For some questions you do not need to do any writing. Instead, they are multiple choice options, ticking the correct answer, drawing lines to, or putting a circle around your answers. It is incredibly important therefore to read the instructions carefully, so that you know how to answer the question. For other questions however, you will need to write a word, phrase or sentence.

The spelling task lasts 15 minutes, although you will be allowed as much time as you need to complete it. Your teacher or another adult will read out twenty sentences. Each sentence has a word missing in the answer booklet. You must listen carefully to the missing word and fill this in, making sure that you spell it correctly. The word will be read out once, then as part of a sentence and then repeated a third and final time.

Test techniques

Before the test

1. When you revise, try revising 'little and often' rather than in long sessions.

2. Read the hints and tips throughout the book to remind you of important points.

3. Revise with a friend. You can encourage and learn from each other.

4. Be prepared – bring your own pens and pencils.

During the test

1. READ THE QUESTION, THEN READ IT AGAIN.

2. If you get stuck, don't linger on the same question – move on! You can come back to it later.

3. Never leave a multiple-choice question. Make an educated guess if you really can't work out the answer.

4. Check to see how many marks a question is worth. Have you 'earned' those marks with your answer?

5. Check your answers after each question. Does your answer look correct?

Where to go to get help

Pages 9, 20, 32 and 49 provide you with a description of what you should aim to do when you are reading and writing at Level 4. You can refer to them at any time to check you are keeping on track to achieve Level 4!

Pages 8–31 are designed to help you improve your writing and include information about writing fiction and non-fiction.

Pages 32–43 will help you give 'voice' to your writing, sharpen up your punctuation and improve your grammar.

Pages 44–45 give you practice in spelling, including a list of key words to learn before your test.

Pages 48–57 are designed to help you succeed in the Reading Test and include reading fiction, non-fiction and poetry.

Page 58 contains the golden rules to improve handwriting.

Page 59 contains a glossary to help you understand key terms about writing, reading and grammar.

Pages 61–63 provide the answers to the practice questions.

Writing non-fiction

Non-fiction texts give you information about something or someone.
They also give you facts and, sometimes, opinions.

Type of non-fiction	Definition and purpose	Where you might read an example
Recount	Tells you about something that has already happened. It may include personal opinions and comments	Letters, diaries, newspapers, biographies, autobiographies, magazines
Instructions and procedures	Tell you how to do something in a step-by-step way	Board game instructions, recipes, directions, how to make or repair something
Non-chronological report	Gives you facts about a topic or subject	Encyclopaedias, information books, posters, leaflets, travel guides
Explanation	Tells you how or why something happens or works	Leaflets, posters, manuals, letters, diagrams, information books
Discussion	Gives you information both for and against a topic	Newspaper articles, letters, magazines, information leaflets, posters, speeches
Persuasion	Tries to influence how you think about someone or something	Advertisements, articles, leaflets, spam emails, letters

Tips	★ Non-fiction writing tasks do not always tell you what text type you need to write. They might just say '*Write an information text …*'
	★ So it is important that you:
	  • think carefully about the *purpose* and *audience* you are writing for. This will help you know what type of text to write
	  • use the correct structure and language features
	  • organise your writing into paragraphs
	  • use connectives thoughtfully
	  • vary the length and type of your sentences
	  • try to be adventurous with your choice of words

Achieve Level 4 writing

At Level 4 your writing is lively and thoughtful. You can develop your ideas and organise them according to the purpose of your writing. You can make adventurous choices of vocabulary and use words for effect. You can use complex sentences, and your spelling and punctuation is usually accurate. Your handwriting is fluent, joined and legible.

Over to you!

- Work through each section and don't rush.
- Learn the purpose of the text type.
- Make sure you understand the way it is organised and the key language features.
- Have a go at the challenges and the practice questions.

Tips	The practice questions
	★ **Decide what the *purpose* of the writing is. This is the clue to which text type to write. E.g.** *Write a letter describing a weekend away ...* **Straight away this tells you the text should be a RECOUNT.** *Write a letter to persuade someone to ...* **Straight away this tells you to write a PERSUASIVE text.** **Get the idea?**	★ **Decide who the *audience* is. This is the clue to what sort of language to include. E.g.** *Write a letter to your best friend ...* **This tells you to use informal language because you know the audience well.** *Write a report for the local museum on ...* **This tells you to use polite, formal language because you don't know exactly who will be reading it.** **Get the idea?**
	ALWAYS READ THE QUESTION AT LEAST TWICE! **Once you have decided on the purpose and audience, plan, write and check your writing.**

Recount

Definition
A recount is a piece of writing that gives information about something that has happened in the past. A recount can include personal feelings and comments.

Purpose
To retell an event or events.

Text plan

1 Introduction — *When* it happened | *Where* it happened | *Who* was involved

2 Events — *What* happened in chronological (time) order

3 Summary — *Why* it happened | *How* someone felt about it

Look at the words in *italics*. You can use these as headings to help you plan a recount.

Think about organising your recount into three paragraphs.

Language features
Events in a recount have already happened, so use verbs in the PAST TENSE, e.g. *We rode to the park* (not *We ride to the park*).

Use TIME CONNECTIVES to link events, e.g. <u>First</u> *we played on the swings.* <u>Next</u> *we fed the ducks.* <u>Later</u> *we had a picnic.*

If you are in the recount, use the FIRST PERSON (*I, we, us*), e.g. <u>We</u> *saw seven white ducks.*

If you are writing about someone else, use the THIRD PERSON (*he, she, they*), e.g. <u>They</u> *went home at 5 o'clock.*

Typical style
Recounts can be INFORMAL when you know the audience, e.g. a personal diary or a letter to a friend.

They can be FORMAL when the audience is unknown, e.g. a newspaper article, a biography or an autobiography.

Challenge
Find and list the time connectives in the News letter text example (page 11).

Tip
★ Recounts can be in the form of a letter, diary entry, biography, autobiography, newspaper article, sports report, news report, email or online blog. Remember to think about the purpose of the text.

Text example

News letter – Our school play

Last Tuesday evening an audience of proud parents crowded into the school hall. They were there to watch the first performance of this year's school play. The play, *The First Letter*, was written by Y6 teacher Miss Reid.

First, the audience was entertained by the school orchestra. They played some tunes and soon many of the parents were singing along. Next, the play started. It was an exciting first half with Robert Higgs in the lead role. Everyone agreed he was fantastic as the cunning Magician. Then it was time for the interval. Drinks and biscuits were served by some of the parents. After a 20-minute break, the play restarted. The audience were on the edge of their seats until the last moment.

Finally the headteacher, Mrs Jones, stood up to

The First Letter
by *Miss Reid*
Starring *Robert Higgs*
as the magician

thank everyone. 'It has been a great success,' she concluded. The audience clapped loudly as Sujata Singh, the youngest pupil, presented Miss Reid with some flowers. As one parent said: 'It was a wonderful evening. I'm really glad I came.'

Practice questions

(1) Write your own personal diary entry about what happened when you went to audition for a school play.

(2) Write an article for the local newspaper describing the local primary school's Christmas pantomime.

HOW DID YOU DO?

Now go back and check your work!

1. This task was to write your diary entry. Usually people keep diaries just for themselves, not for the whole world to read, so the audience was you. This means that it should have been informal with brief language. Did you use past tense verbs? Did you use brief language? (See page 61 for an example answer.)

2. This task was to write a recount in the form of a newspaper article. The audience was the general public. This means that it should be quite a formal piece of writing with some interesting information and written in the third person. As the readers might not know the people in the article, did you explain who they were? Did you use past tense verbs? Did you use time connectives to order your ideas? Did you organise your writing into paragraphs?

Instructions and procedures

Achieved? ☺ 😐 ☹

Definition
Instructions tell the reader how to do, make or play something or how to get somewhere.

Purpose
To instruct.

Text plan

1 Aim

2 What you need

3 What you do

This is the title and tells the reader what the instructions are about.

A list of the things that are needed to achieve the aim. These are listed in order of use.

A step-by-step chronological (time order) sequence of what to do achieve the aim.

So, usually in instructions there is a title and two headings.

You need to decide on the best headings for the instructions you are writing.

A recipe could have *Ingredients* and *Method* as the headings.

Language features
Use amounts and quantities in the list of things that are needed, e.g.

   3 counters   1 dice   1 pack of cards

You must write in the PRESENT TENSE. If you start to slip into the past tense, you are writing a recount!

Use commands or the IMPERATIVE VOICE. Put the verb at the beginning of the sentence, e.g. *Cut the paper into a circle.*

Write in the SECOND PERSON. Instructions are talking directly to the reader but you don't need to use the word 'you', e.g. 'Cut the paper.' not 'You cut the paper.

Use CONNECTIVES that are time related e.g. *first, secondly, finally.*

Sometimes you might need to tell the reader how to carry out the instruction by using adverbs, e.g. *Carefully cut the paper.* The adverb can go before the verb at the beginning of the sentence.

You can use bullet points to help the reader.

Typical style
Use BRIEF LANGUAGE. The reader doesn't want lots of words to wade through if they are following instructions. Be careful not to overload sentences with detail.

Tip ★ Think 'step-by-step'. This will help you to order your writing.

Text example

How to look after a pet dinosaur

What you need

A large garden or open space

Plenty of trees and shrubs

Fresh water

Sturdy container, e.g. bath

Scale polish

Lead

1 Your dinosaur needs plenty of room to roam. Allow him time to explore his new home. Keep an eye on him from a distance.

2 Feed your dinosaur on a regular basis by giving him plenty of fresh leaves and other greenery. Offer several litres of fresh water each day in a container that cannot easily be knocked over.

3 Gently clean the dinosaur with scale polish about twice a week. His skin should look supple.

4 Carefully place a lead around his neck in order to take him out in public. Teach him to follow you and to come when you call.

5 Take care of him and you will have a happy life with your pet dinosaur.

Practice questions

1 You know where there is some buried treasure on a small island in the middle of an ocean. A brave explorer has offered to go and get the treasure for you. Write some instructions that tell him where to find it.

2 The aliens have landed and want to come to school! Write a set of instructions telling the aliens how to get dressed for school so that they will blend in with the rest of the pupils.

HOW DID YOU DO?

Now go back and check your work!

1. This task was to write a set of instructions in the form of directions. The audience was a brave explorer looking for some buried treasure. This means that he would need detailed information about how to get to the treasure. You could have told him what landmarks to look out for on the route. Did you think about what he would need to take with him? You could have listed things like a rope and a spade.

2. This task was to write a set of instructions for getting dressed for school. The audience was a group of aliens. They would not be familiar with the names of human clothing nor how to put it on. You would need to describe clothes very carefully and give detailed instructions about how to put the clothes on. (See page 61 for an example answer.)

Non-chronological report

Definition
Non-chronological reports give a reader information about something or somewhere. They are usually about a group of things, e.g. *dinosaurs*, not one thing in particular, e.g. *Dilly the dinosaur*. Facts about the subject are organised into paragraphs.

Purpose
To give information.

Text plan

1 Title — Usually the subject of the report.

2 Introduction — Definition of the subject.

3 Series of paragraphs about various aspects of the subject — Facts usually grouped by topic.

4 Summary or rounding-off statement — Could be an unusual fact about the subject.

Paragraphs are the key to writing non-chronological reports. Try to use at least two paragraphs after the introduction and before the rounding-off statement.

Decide what each paragraph is going to be about and only have that information in there.

Language features
Use the PRESENT TENSE if the subject still exists, e.g. *Crocoraffes have, are, live*. Use the PAST TENSE if the subject is from the past, e.g. *Dinosaurs were, had, lived*.

Use TECHNICAL VOCABULARY (language about the subject), e.g. *Many dinosaurs were <u>herbivores</u>*.

Use FACTUAL ADJECTIVES to give more information about a fact, e.g. *They had <u>very sharp</u> teeth and <u>strong</u> jaws*.

Challenge
Write a key word to summarise each of the paragraphs in the text example on page 13.

Typical style
Use IMPERSONAL sentence starts, e.g. sentences that begin with *The crocoraffes ..., They are ..., It is ..., Crocoraffes ...*

Sentences that begin with *I, she, he, we* are personal sentence starts.

Remember always to use IMPERSONAL sentences.

Tip ★ Reports can be in the form of letters, encyclopaedia entries, information posters or leaflets, as well as straightforward pieces of writing.

Text example

Crocoraffes

Crocoraffes are large animals. They can breathe and eat, both in and out of water. They were discovered on 1 April 2008 by the explorer Sir Humbert Bumbert while he was trekking through dense jungle.

Crocoraffes are about the size of a large horse and have scaly skin that has a mottled effect. They have long necks, which they use to reach up into the highest branches for leaves. They also have very sharp teeth and strong jaws in order to catch their prey when swimming under water. The animal's broad muscular legs push it quickly through water.

Crocoraffes are omnivores. This means that they eat both leaves and meat. They are attracted by the tender new shoots of the honey tree and can cause considerable damage to these trees. In the water, crocoraffes will catch and eat up to fifty large fish in a day.

The jungles of South America appear to be the only place where crocoraffes can be found. They keep to the thickest part of the jungle that is rarely, if ever, visited by people. They make large nests from jungle creepers and line them with mud from the river bank. This hardens to create a sturdy home for a pair of crocoraffes and their offspring.

They can live for as long as forty to fifty years and mate for life. During this partnership a couple can produce as many as a hundred offspring, known as crocoraffettes.

Practice questions

(1) Your task is to write a leaflet to display outside the main enclosure of Sir Humbert Bumbert's Butterfly Farm that houses all the rare and unusual butterfly species he has collected on his travels.

(2) The fossilised skeleton of a newly discovered type of dinosaur has been found. Your task is to write a poster to display in a children's museum to tell visitors about this type of dinosaur.

HOW DID YOU DO?

Now go back and check your work!

1. The task was to write a report in the form of a leaflet. The leaflet will be displayed at the Butterfly Farm, so the audience would be the general public. This means that you needed to write in a formal style. In the introduction you should have briefly described what a butterfly farm is and what you can see there. In the next two or three paragraphs you should have chosen different things to write about in more detail, e.g. types of butterfly, habitat, life-cycle. Did you use present tense verbs? You should not have included very much about

2. Your task was to write a report in the form of a poster. This will be displayed at a children's museum so the audience is the general public, but as it is mainly for young people you could have used a slightly informal style. Did you still have the information organised into paragraphs? As this report was in the form of a poster, you should have used brief language. Did you use, for example, bullet points, tables or charts? (See page 61 for an example answer.)

how and where they were found or it will turn into a recount before your very eyes!

Explanation

Definition
An explanation tells the reader how or why something works or happens. It can be about natural things, e.g. *why volcanoes erupt*, or about mechanical things, e.g. *how a radio works*.

Purpose
To explain.

Text plan

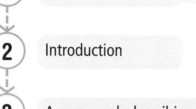

1 Title

2 Introduction

3 A paragraph describing the parts and/or appearance of the subject or process to be explained

4 A paragraph explaining what something does, or why or how it works, often in time order

5 Concluding paragraph

Tells the reader what the explanation is about. Often contains *how* or *why*.

Tells the reader about the subject or process of the explanation.

Summarising or rounding off. This could include where the subject or process occurs, or its effects.

Language features
Use PRESENT TENSE verbs, e.g. *Ships carry goods.* Use PAST TENSE verbs for historical topics, e.g. *Pirate ships were common.*

Use TIME-BASED CONNECTIVES to show the order in which things happen, e.g. *first, next, finally.*

Use CAUSE AND EFFECT CONNECTIVES to show how one thing makes something else happen, e.g. *as, so that, in order to, because, this results in.*

Use TECHNICAL VOCABULARY (specific language for the subject), e.g. *When the wind blows, the angle of the sails make the ship tack.*

EXPLAIN technical terms if need be. You can define terms in the text, or write a glossary, e.g. *tack: sail into the wind using a zig-zag pattern.*

Typical style
The PASSIVE VOICE, e.g. *Sometimes travellers were captured by pirates*, can make the explanation more formal. Remember to use a variety of sentence types.

Tip ★ Explanations can be in the form of letters, diagrams, information leaflets, encyclopaedia entries and posters.

Text example

How pirates attack! (from *How to be a successful pirate!*)

Pirate ships attack any merchant vessel they think might contain valuable goods or money. If the pirate ship is a well-armed large vessel this does not present a problem, but in reality, pirate ships are not big or well armed.

So how can a small pirate ship overcome a larger vessel that has superior fire-power and a crew that outnumbers them? The main tactics used by pirates should be speed and surprise.

When a ship is seen in the distance, the pirate captain studies it through his telescope and makes an assessment of how far away it is and what booty it contains. He then orders the crew to set the sails to make maximum speed towards the vessel. When the pirates are closer to the target, they slow down and attempt to fool the larger vessel into thinking their ship is harmless. Often they raise the same flag so they appear to come from the same country. Sometimes they even send a distress message using the ship's flags. When the pirates are so close that the other ship cannot escape, they throw off their disguise and raise the Jolly Roger.

Even then, you might think, a ship with a much larger crew and armed with many more cannons would easily be able to resist the attack. Therefore, in order to overcome larger, better armed ships, pirates rely heavily on fear! They swarm onto the deck of the target, shouting and screaming, firing guns with clouds of smoke and creating as much noise and chaos as possible. The famous pirate 'Blackbeard' even has lighted fuses tied in his hair. He looks so fearsome that often crews surrender without putting up any fight at all. All this quick action usually means that the captured crew are defeated.

Next, the pirate captain offers a deal to the captives: they can join the pirates or be thrown overboard! It is not surprising that many captured seamen become pirates themselves.

Practice questions

(1) You have invented a system to stop pirates from being able to board ships. Shipping companies that have lost their cargo to pirates want to know all about it. Write an article for *Shipping Magazine* explaining how it works.

(2) Your class has invented a new type of lunch box! Write a letter from your teacher to the parents of your class, explaining how this works.

HOW DID YOU DO?

Now go back and check your work!

1. This task was to write an explanation in the form of a magazine article. The audience would be the owners of shipping companies, so the article would be formal in style. Did you use paragraphs? Did you use cause and effect language? If you have used past tense verbs, then it has turned into a recount! If you wrote telling the shipping companies how to work the system themselves, then it has turned into instructions!

2. This task was to write an explanation in the form of a letter from your teacher to the parents. (See page 61 for an example answer.)

Discussion

☺ ☹ ☹

Definition
A discussion text or *balanced argument* gives the reader information about an issue from different points of view. Readers are left to make up their own minds about how they feel about the issue.

Purpose
To present opposing points of view about an issue.

Text plan

1	Title	Often in the form of a question.
2	Identifying the issue	Opening paragraph states and explains what the issue is and briefly introduces the main arguments.
3	Points in support of the issue	Arguments for, with supporting evidence.
4	Points opposing the issue	Arguments against, with supporting evidence. You can also use argument/counter-argument, one point at a time.
5	Concluding paragraph	Summarising or rounding off. This sometimes recommends one point of view.

Language features
You can use PRESENT TENSE verbs or the PAST TENSE depending on the issue.

Use LOGICAL CONNECTIVES to organise your argument, e.g. *therefore, consequently, so.*

Use connectives that show the OPPOSITE view, e.g. *on the one hand, on the other hand, but, however, nevertheless.*

Use a CONNECTIVE in the final paragraph to signal that you are SUMMING UP, e.g. *in conclusion, to summarise, finally.*

Use EVIDENCE and EXAMPLES to support the points made. These could be numbers and statistics, facts or quotes.

Typical style
Use an IMPERSONAL STYLE. Say what <u>people</u> think, not what <u>you</u> think. Use the PASSIVE VOICE, e.g. *It is thought that, it is believed.*

Challenge
Find and list the passive verb phrases in the discussion on page 19.

Tip	★ Remember to keep your argument balanced. Write four or five points for, and four or five points against.

Text example

How should pirates be punished?

Everyone agrees that piracy is the greatest problem to our merchant ships this century. Pirates plunder our ships, steal their cargoes, capture our sailors and frequently kill them. Everybody involved in sea-travel seems to have a horror story about pirates.

Recently, there has been a great deal of publicity about what to do to about it. It seems most people think any pirates that are caught should immediately be hanged. People argue that this would act as a warning to others. It would show the young, the poor, beggars and thieves that piracy only leads to one outcome – death. They also argue that pirates don't deserve anything else.

However, there are others who believe that *everyone* has the right to a trial. It is a well-known fact that many seamen have been forced to become pirates when they were themselves captured. The number of unwilling pirates is believed to be as high as 45%. Therefore, hanging pirates without a trial could mean that many innocent victims would suffer. A spokesperson for PAPT (Pirates Are People Too!) stated recently: 'These pirate-victims would return to an ordinary way of life if given the chance and would become decent citizens.' Consequently, they believe *all* pirates should be given a chance. The ones who decide to give up piracy could also give important information about the others and this could help put an end to piracy altogether.

On the other hand, most people believe such a soft approach would result in more pirates, not fewer.

It has been shown that swift and strong punishment has led to a reduction in petty theft by pick-pockets and others. This may also prove to be the case with piracy.

Whatever the final conclusion, it is clear that this issue is complex and needs detailed discussion by Parliament before a solution can be found.

Practice questions

(1) There has been a huge increase in the amount of graffiti on the streets of your town. Some examples of the graffiti are beautifully drawn and coloured, others are just scribble. Your task is to write a TV news report to prompt discussion about what should be done, both to the graffiti artists and to the graffiti itself.

(2) Write a summary using bullet points to help a speaker set the scene for a discussion on 'Should mobile phones be allowed in school?'

HOW DID YOU DO?

Now go back and check your work!

1. This task was to write a discussion in the form of a TV news report. The audience is the general public, so your writing should be fairly formal. Even though it would be a spoken news report, the issue is important to the audience, so did you organise your points clearly in paragraphs? Did you balance points for and against the issue?

2. This task was to write a discussion in bullet point form to summarise the issue and provide someone with notes about it. Did you identify the issue? Did you write your points briefly, but remember to give some supporting evidence? (See page 61 for an example answer.)

Persuasion

Definition
A persuasive text tries to make the reader think, do or buy something.

Purpose
To persuade.

Text plan

1 Identify the main point of the text

Could be a statement or question to grab the reader's attention.

2 Supporting points

Organise the reasons into a paragraph for each point with supporting evidence. Explain how people are being affected by the situation.

3 Summary of key points

Repeat the key points to reinforce them.

4 Call to action

Ask the reader to take some action, e.g. to do something, to buy something, to think something, to go somewhere.

Language features
Normally the PRESENT TENSE is used, but you could move into the past or future depending on the point being made.

Support the reasons with EVIDENCE. This could be numbers and statistics, facts or quotes.

Appeal to your readers' emotions by using EMOTIVE LANGUAGE. Make them think about how what you are saying affects them. Try to make them feel something with words, e.g. *It all costs money and who pays for it? You do!*

Include lots of detail in order to explain your ideas clearly and you will be more persuasive.

Typical style
Use the PASSIVE VOICE if you don't want to say where you are getting your evidence from, e.g. *It is thought ... It is believed ... Studies have shown ...*

Challenge
How many passive verb phrases can you find in the text on page 21? If you can use one or two passive verbs, you will get better marks, but don't overdo it!

Tip

★ **Persuasive texts can be in virtually any form. They can be letters, posters, leaflets, newspaper and magazine articles or adverts. Remember to think about the *purpose* of the text. Remember to think about who the *audience* is and which words you choose.**

Text example

> Dear Mr Jones,
>
> I am writing to complain about the quality of the school dinners on offer recently at St Starvin's Primary School.
>
> There have been no fresh fruit or vegetables offered for the last two weeks. Also the chips and nuggets are always very greasy and unappetising. The standard of desserts is also poor – we have had prunes and semolina every day for a month.
>
> As a result of this a number of Year 6 pupils have refused to eat their lunch and have been tired and unable to concentrate in the afternoons.
>
> It has been proven that five portions of fresh fruit and vegetables should be eaten every day to keep people healthy, particularly children. Studies have also shown that protein eaten at lunch time has the effect of boosting brain-power for the rest of the day. Our National Tests begin in May and many of us are very concerned that our results will suffer as a result of this poor diet! This, of course, would have a very bad effect on the reputation of the school.
>
> Although a small number of pupils enjoy your fried food, the majority of us are keen to maintain a balanced diet and lead a healthy lifestyle.
>
> Could you please provide us with suggestions for alternative menus? A group of us would be happy to help with this as we have many ideas ourselves.
>
> I look forward to hearing from you soon.
>
> Yours sincerely,
>
> Em T. Tum, Class 6D

Practice questions

(1) Your class has been told that there won't be any school trips for them this year, due to lack of funds. Write a letter to the school governors to persuade them to hold more fundraising events.

(2) Your school football team is short of players. Write a poster to advertise a try-out session after school.

HOW DID YOU DO?

Now go back and check your work!

1. This task was to write a persuasive text in the form of a letter. The audience was the school governors. This means that the tone of the letter should be formal. You need to have thought carefully about your point of view and how to appeal to the governors, and supported your point of view with reasons and evidence. Did you organise your letter into paragraphs? Did you reinforce your main point by repetition? Did you ask the governors to take action?

2. This task was to write a persuasive text in the form of a poster. The audience was other children in your school so the tone could be informal. Did you include key information and brief language? Did you remember to attract the readers' attention and use language that appealed to the audience? (See page 61 for an example answer.)

Writing fiction

Fiction texts can be in the form of stories, plays or poetry. The main purpose of fiction is to entertain a reader. It can also make readers think about a theme or an issue, or teach a lesson or moral.

In this section we will concentrate on writing stories.

There are three things that all stories have in common:

Setting   Characters   Theme

Page 23 of this book looks at the way stories are structured.

Page 24 looks at these story 'ingredients'. You need to put all three into the mixture to make a story.

There is a section on each of the ingredients on pages 25–28. Each section provides you with tips, ideas and examples. There are also some practice questions. These are short writing tasks.

Stories need planning! On pages 30 and 31 you will find ideas to help you plan. Planning is important, so don't skip this bit!

Over to you!
- Work through each section carefully.
- Make sure you understand what you want your reader to think or feel.
- Have a go at the practice questions.
- Look back at the section. Have you included the right sort of detail in the right sort of way?

Achieve Level 4 Writing
At Level 4 your writing is lively and thoughtful. You can develop your ideas and organise them according to the purpose of your writing. You can make adventurous choices of vocabulary and use words for effect. You can use a variety of sentence types including complex sentences, and your spelling and punctuation is usually accurate. Your handwriting is fluent, joined and legible.

Tips	★ All writers 'borrow' ideas from other writers, so read as much as you can! Note down ideas, sentences, phrases and words that you like. Use them in your own writing. ★ Keep a 'writing ideas' book. ★ Your reader doesn't know what is happening inside your head while you write, so make sure you tell or show them. ★ When your characters are talking, tell the reader who is speaking. ★ Use paragraphs. Think *Person, Time, Place* (PTP). When the person, time or place changes in your story, start a new paragraph.

Story structure

All stories are organised in the same basic way.

When you plan your story, think in five sections:

1 Beginning | **Introduce the setting and the main characters.**

2 Build-up | **The story gets going. The characters start to do something.**

3 Problem | **Something goes wrong! This is the most exciting part of the story.**

4 Resolution | **The problem gets sorted out.**

5 Ending | **All the loose ends are tied up. The characters think or reflect on what has happened.**

Setting, characters and theme

Before you plan your story, you need to decide on the three main ingredients: setting, characters and theme.

Setting

This is WHEN and WHERE your story takes place. You need to help your readers make a picture in their minds. The setting can also be used to create an atmosphere and affect how the reader feels.

Think about some of the stories you have read. When and where were they set? How do you know? Look at some short stories to see how the authors have told the reader about the setting. Have a go at drawing the setting that you read about.

There is more about story settings on page 25.

Characters

This is WHO is in the story. You need to help the readers build up a picture of the characters – not just APPEARANCE but also PERSONALITY. Your readers need to have an idea of what the characters are like.

Think about the stories you have read. Who were the characters? What were they like? How do you know? What were they called? How did they speak? Look at some short stories to see how authors have told the reader about the characters. Try drawing a character as you see them in your mind's eye.

There is more about character on page 26 and more about dialogue (how characters speak) on page 29.

Theme

This is WHAT happens in the story. Some people say that there are only a few story themes in the world. All writers borrow ideas from other stories and this is something you can do.

Think about stories you have read. What happened? Did one story remind you of any others? List some of the common themes, e.g. good overcomes evil, main character loses something.

There is more about theme on page 28.

Once you have chosen your ingredients, mix them together and make a story!

Setting

Introduce the setting in the beginning section of the story. Remember, the two things you need to tell your readers are *when* and *where* the story is set.

When and where?

The big picture

Is your story set in the past, now or in the future? Look at these three examples. How has the writer told the reader about the big picture?

The spaceship hovered near the planet, waiting for cargo-ships to leave the surface.

Black Jake stuffed his cutlass through his belt, straightened his tricorn hat and began to stride across the quarter deck.

Jon eagerly put his new Harry Potter DVD into the player and pressed Play.

Above, this writer has used objects to tell us when and where the story is set. Spaceships and planets point to the story being set in the future. A cutlass, tri-corn hat and quarter deck tell us this story is probably set in the past. The DVD shows us that the story is set in the present day.

The smaller picture

Writers tell us more about the setting by adding smaller details. Look how the writer tells us about the season when the story takes place.

Twists of dust rose in the heat of the planet's surface as it moved towards the blazing sun.

Black Jake shielded his eyes as the snowflakes grew thicker and peered into the murky distance.

Jon settled down to enjoy the next hour and ignored the rain and wind as they lashed the last of the leaves from the trees outside.

This is a more interesting way than just saying *It was very hot ...* or *It was a cold winter day ...* or *On a wet autumn afternoon ...*

Characters

Introduce your main characters at the beginning of the story. Have a picture of them in your mind. Three things that will make your characters 'real' are:
- what they look like
- what they say and how they say it
- how they move.

What they look like

You can describe the characters' face, hair and clothes.

What do you think the two characters below are like? How has the writer made you feel that way?

Jack strode to the window, his long black coat flapping around his strong legs. A deep frown creased his forehead and his eyes narrowed dangerously beneath the brim of his hat.	*Her wild tangled hair was only half-tamed by the bits of twine tied into it. Her clothes had seen better days; torn striped breeches and an old lace shirt; but she stood straight and tall as any great lady of society.*

Challenge 1

The descriptions above tell us something about the characters' appearance. What else has the writer told us about these characters?

Tip	★ Make sure your descriptions are *important* to your character. Don't waste words when they are not needed in the story!

What they say and how they say it

Dialogue adds interest and variety to your writing. But dialogue needs to move the story along. What has the writer done in these two extracts?

Jack strode to the window, his long black coat flapping around his strong legs. A deep frown creased his forehead and his eyes narrowed dangerously beneath the brim of his hat. 'Who laughed?' he growled angrily.	*Her wild tangled hair was only half-tamed by the bits of twine tied into it. Her clothes had seen better days; torn striped breeches and an old lace shirt; but she stood straight and tall as any great lady of society. 'Stay where you are!' she cried, her voice trembling.*

The writer has added dialogue that tells us what the characters said, but also how they said it by using powerful speech verbs and adverbs.

How they move

Describing how the characters move helps to bring your writing to life. What words has the author used in the extracts above to describe the movement of the characters?

Challenge 2

Write a paragraph describing in your own words how you feel about each of these two characters. Look for *clues* in the descriptions. Think about:

- Appearance – why do they look the way they do?
- Dialogue – what does the dialogue tell you about each character's feelings and personality?
- Movement – what does the way they move tell you about the characters?

Tips	★ Keep to two or three characters only. If you have two characters, make one male and one female, then there is no confusion about pronouns (*he/she*). ★ Only use dialogue when it tells the reader more about the character or the plot. Don't waste words on idle chat. ★ Don't tell your reader everything. Give clues!

Practice questions

1 Old Ben is a very old sailor who is grumpy. His age and experience make him short-tempered with younger sailors. Write a description of how he eats his breakfast on the deck of a busy ship. Remember to give readers clues through action, appearance and dialogue. Give clues – don't tell. Include details about what else is happening around him as he eats, and how he shows his grumpiness and short temper with the younger sailors.

2 Your best friend is an astronaut. Write a description of her when you meet her as she lands from her latest space mission.

Theme

Most stories have simple themes:
- Good beats bad
- Lost and found
- Wishing or wanting.

Challenge 1

Which theme do you think belongs to these well-known stories? Discuss your answers with friends or your teacher.

- *The Lord of the Rings*

- *Harry Potter*

- *Cinderella*

Basic structure
Good overcomes evil.

(1)	Beginning	Two characters – one good, one evil. Setting.
(2)	Build-up	Evil character plots against good character. Good character is innocently unaware.
(3)	Problem	Evil character tricks or threatens to harm good character.
(4)	Resolution	Good character outwits evil character.
(5)	Ending	Everything is OK. Characters reflect or think about what has happened.

Once you've got the hang of the structure you can start to experiment. You might write a story about a person overcoming a fear or a bully. It's still a similar structure.

Challenge 2

Can you use a grid like this to work out how the themes of **lost and found** and **wishing or wanting** follow the plan?

Now try it with other stories you know.

Dialogue

A story without any dialogue could be very dull. *What* characters say and *how* they say it can tell readers a lot about the characters in a story *and* move the plot along.

Use powerful speech verbs to tell your readers about the character who is speaking.

Consider these examples:
1. *The stranger stood in front of me. 'Move,' he muttered.*
2. *The stranger stood in front of me. 'Move!' he shouted.*
3. *The stranger stood in front of me. 'Move,' he pleaded.*
4. *The stranger stood in front of me. 'Move!' he screamed.*

How do the different speech verbs affect your thoughts:
a) about the character of the stranger?
b) about the plot?

'move...'

'Move!'

'move!'

Challenge

Write a sentence to suggest why 'the stranger' said '*Move*' in each of the four different ways.

'Said' is the speech verb that is used the most but it doesn't tell readers anything about character or plot. Use it when you do not need to add extra detail.

Try to use a variety of powerful and common speech verbs. Don't overuse powerful verbs.

Tips	★ Dialogue needs to move the story along. Only use it when you want to tell the reader something important about the setting, characters or plot. ★ Try to use a variety of verbs *and* adverbs to show how characters are speaking.

Grammar and punctuation in dialogue

Make it very clear who is speaking. When a new person joins the dialogue, always start their spoken words on a new line.

Use pronouns (*he/she/they*) and the characters' names. See pages 38–39 for further information about punctuation and punctuating dialogue.

Planning

Planning is a very useful way of thinking about story ingredients and organising your ideas. It makes sense to develop a way of planning that is fast and works for you.

Try using the five-box plan below. Make sure you know the heading for each box and the main things that need to be in that section of the story.

Heading	Main things to include	Example
Beginning	Introduce main character Setting	Joe, boy about 11, into skateboarding. Old empty house, bit spooky.
Build-up	Story gets going	Joe goes into house. Looking for something. Sees paw prints.
Problem	Something goes wrong	Can hear cat but can't get to it. Cat stuck behind wall.
Resolution	Problems sorted out	Joe finds secret button to open wall. Rescues cat.
Ending	Loose ends tied up Characters reflect or think	Everything OK. Joe and cat go off on skateboard.

Now it's just a case of turning your plan into a story. But please remember to refer to your plan while you are writing – don't write something completely different!

1. Practise quickly drawing out the five-box plan and adding the headings. This should take no more than 30 seconds!
2. Now look back at the main things to include. Practise adding the main things to your five boxes. This should take another 30 seconds.
3. Next, practise planning actual stories (you don't need to write them at this stage). Look at some of the Practice questions on page 31. Read the task carefully, then reread it. Got an idea? Go!
4. Think about the story ingredients you could include. Remember – **setting, characters, theme**. Spend no more than 4 minutes on this. You've now used up 5 minutes of your planning time.
5. Make notes about the ingredients in the boxes. Remember, these are notes, not sentences! You are not writing the story here – you are planning it. Five minutes later – time's up!

Tips	★ Read the task carefully first. Then make notes. Think *setting, characters, theme*. Don't write sentences – you are not writing the story yet, just making a plan. ★ A well-planned story is better than one that rambles and ends abruptly.

Putting it all together

So, you know the three story ingredients (setting, characters, theme), you know the structure and you know how to plan (five-box plan). It's just a case of putting it all together in a short story.

Look at the example below. It includes all the story ingredients that you have been reading about.

The empty house

Joe pushed open the huge wooden door into a large stone-floored hallway. He slipped through the doorway, cobwebs brushing his face. Once inside he breathed in the musty, damp smell of the old empty house.

'Hello!' he called. 'Is anyone there?' All he heard was his own voice echoing around the hall. Looking at the floor he could see paw prints in the dust. He moved forward, tracking them like a hunter in the desert. Then, suddenly, they stopped. Joe found himself staring at a blank wall. There were no more paw prints to be seen.

'Cinders can't have disappeared into thin air,' he muttered. 'Cats don't do that.'

He paused and held his breath. He thought he could hear a faint meowing. He listened hard. His black eyes stood out in his pale face as he knelt down on the floor and put his ear to the wall. Finally his face brightened as he started tapping at the wall.

With a creak, a panel in the wall started to move. The meowing grew louder and Joe's smile grew wider. Eventually the gap in the wall was big enough to reveal … Cinders, Joe's little black cat.

'Oh Cinders, how did you get in there?' asked Joe. Cinders arched her back and purred.

'Come on, let's go,' Joe said. He picked up his skateboard as the pair left the empty house. Placing it on the ground, he patted the front. Cinders jumped on and sat up straight, looking like the proudest cat in town. Joe hopped on behind her and they sped off down the street.

'That's the last time I let you go mouse hunting in there!' Joe told his cat. Cinders blinked and didn't make a sound.

Practice questions

Remember to think, plan, write and check your writing.

1. You are in a big shopping centre with your dad and little sister. Continue the story after this opening sentence, *'Where's little Mari?' asked Dad …*

2. Write a story with this title: 'The mystery of the missing garden gnome'.

3. Write a story that could end with this sentence: *'Jamal knew that Butch Brown would never scare him again.'*

4. Write a story with these ingredients: a black cat, an old woman, a scary wood, good overcomes evil.

5. Write a story about a girl who wants to star in the school play.

Grammar

Now you know how to organise your writing for non-fiction and for stories, you know what to include and what to leave out.

> Polishing up your grammar could make the final difference to your writing.

In a Level 4 piece of writing, the writer needs to:
* use different types of SENTENCE and PUNCTUATE them correctly
* organise writing into PARAGRAPHS
* use a variety of suitable CONNECTIVES
* choose VOCABULARY carefully.

Tip	★ **When you are reading, look carefully at how writers use grammar. Remember, you can 'borrow' their ideas and use them in your own writing.**

Remember, to achieve Level 4 you need to use different types of sentence and punctuate them correctly.

> • Sentences start with a capital letter and end with a full stop (.), question mark (?) or exclamation mark (!).
>
> • A sentence is made up of one or more clauses.
>
> • There are three main types of sentence – simple, compound and complex. You can use them in different ways to have an effect on your reader.

Three types of sentence

Simple sentences

As the name suggests, simple sentences are easy to write and read. They have one clause: *It was raining.*

Using lots of simple sentences can be very boring for a reader.

I went out. It was raining hard. I put up my brolly. I saw my friend Daisy. I called loudly to her. She came over.

These sentences aren't very interesting for a reader because they are all the same length.

Challenge 1

Can you write your own simple sentence?

Compound sentences

Compound sentences have two or more clauses that are as important as each other. They can be joined by these connectives:

and but so

It was raining hard <u>so</u> I put up my brolly.

| Tips | ★ Be careful that you don't always use *and* to join two clauses. |
| | ★ Learn the connectives in the list so that you can use all of them. |

Challenge 2

Can you make your simple sentence into a compound sentence?

Complex sentences

Complex sentences have two or more clauses, but one clause is more important than the others. This is called the *main clause*. A less important clause is called a *subordinate clause*. A subordinate clause is linked to the main clause by a connective:

E.g. *after   although   as   because   before   if   in case*
      once   since   though   unless   until   when   while

When I left the house, I found it was raining hard so I put up my brolly.

Challenge 3

Try making your compound sentence into a complex sentence.

Mixing sentences

If you always use the same type of sentence, your writing will become boring. You need to use a mix.

Look again at these simple sentences.

I went out. It was raining hard. I put up my brolly. I saw my friend Daisy. I called loudly to her. She came over.

How can they be improved?

I went out. It was raining hard so I put up my brolly. As I was struggling with the catch, I saw my friend Daisy. I called loudly to her. She came over, splashing through the puddles on her way.

Well, that sounds better, doesn't it? Can you spot what's changed? Changing the sentence type means that the reader is given more detail, too.

Using questions

You can have your characters asking questions when they are speaking, but try asking questions in other parts of the story as well.

- *Hanif could just see something through the mist, but what was it?*
- *Why was the table shaking?*
- *How would Jake get out of this fix?*
- *Where were they to go now?*

Asking questions means that the reader asks them too and becomes more interested in the story.

Using exclamations

You can have your characters exclaiming when they speak. You can also use exclamations to make part of a story more interesting.

- *It spoke!*
- *She was stuck!*
- *He jumped!*
- *I was dumbstruck!*

How do they do it?

Let's look at how two children's authors use different sentence types.

The locket

He didn't look back. He set sail into the night, delighted with his daring exploits and laughing with excitement at the thought of the riches he knew would be his. Halfway into his voyage home, he could contain himself no longer and he opened the locket.

The author has used all three sentence types in this extract.

Secrets and eyes

My thirst satisfied, I looked down at the boy in faded Bermuda shorts who had taken my money. He looked at me cautiously with eyes that held the secrets of someone twice his age.

In this extract the author starts a sentence with a subordinate clause.

Challenge 4

Identify a simple sentence, a compound sentence and a complex sentence in the extract 'The locket'.

Practice questions

1. Using *The locket* extract, write a paragraph about the character. Write about where the character had been and what he had done.

2. Describe the contents of the locket and the character's reaction to it using a compound sentence. Use a simple sentence to keep the reader in suspense.

Challenge 5

Continue the story *Secrets and eyes* using a variety of types and lengths of sentence.

Tips	★ Look at books in your classroom and find examples of how authors use different sentence types in their writing.
	★ Try using some of their sentences as models for your own writing.

35

Types of connectives

Remember, when you write you should use a variety of suitable connectives.

Connectives are words and phrases that link ideas (clauses) and sentences or introduce new paragraphs.

If you look back at the non-fiction section on pages 8–21, the types of connective that you can use for different text types are listed.

There are different connectives for different purposes.

You need to know what a connective means before you can use it. It is very tempting to impress a marker with higher-level connectives, but this can happen:

Hope put her coat *and* her scarf on. *Furthermore* she put on her boots. *Meanwhile* her friends came round. *On the other hand* they went to the park.

Although the above paragraph uses Level 4 connectives, it is not fluent and the connectives do not make sense.

Challenge

Rewrite the above paragraph using connectives that make sense.

Tip	★ When you are reading, make a note of the connectives the author has used. Think about how they have moved the story along.

Try to remember connectives in these groups:

Instead of using 'and' – to add extra information		To show time passing – instructions, story writing	
• also • as well as • moreover • too		• next • first, second, third… • meanwhile • after	• then • finally • eventually • before
To emphasise or stress your point – arguments, discussion		**Comparing connectives – to compare ideas, arguments, discussion**	
• above all • especially • indeed	• in particular • significantly • notably	• equally • similarly • as with	• in the same way • likewise • like
To explain a point – explanations, arguments, reports		**To show something might happen**	
• because • therefore • consequently	• so • thus	• however • unless • if	• although • except • as long as
To introduce a point – arguments, persuasion		**To contrast and compare – discussion, arguments**	
• for example • for instance • in the case of	• such as • as revealed by	• whereas • alternatively • unlike	• instead of • otherwise • on the other hand

Tips	★ Don't use the same connective over and over again in one piece of writing. ★ Make a list of connectives and learn them. ★ Collect new connectives from your reading.

Challenge

Use these three connectives to make compound sentences from the following simple sentences: a) *because* b) *although* c) *until*

1. *The attack began well. They had been warned of our approach.*
2. *The waves continued crashing on the decks. Everything below was soaked through.*
3. *He stopped running. His heart wasn't in it any more.*

Punctuation

Punctuation tells your reader *how* to read your writing.

Without simple punctuation, your writing will be confusing to read and difficult to understand.

Although full stops and capital letters are the first features of punctuation that we learn, they are often the ones we forget.

> Read these words out loud. How does the punctuation change the meaning?
>
> *Now.   Now!   Now?   Now ...*

Whilst trying to use different types of punctuation, we must remember to check and edit what we write, ensuring that full stops and capital letters are used correctly.

Level 4 writers need to use a range of punctuation marks, but it is not a competition to use the most features. Putting brackets, commas, speech marks and question marks into a paragraph will not automatically make it a Level 4 paragraph.

Challenge

Correct the errors in this paragraph.

Mr Walsh was having an awful day. It was windy and wet (so everybody) was inside for lunch time. The children were behaving, like wild animals and the classroom looked like a zoo?

TRICKY PUNCTUATION

Commas

A comma is a punctuation mark that separates part of a sentence.
Use commas to:

1. separate items in a list, e.g.
   Don't forget your football boots, shin pads, water bottle and towel.

2. add extra information, (brackets and dashes can also do this job), e.g.
   Freddie really enjoyed swimming, in the sea, with his Mum and Dad.

3. separate subordinate clauses, e.g.
   In order to pay for her holiday, Claire had to save over a thousand pounds.

SPEECH PUNCTUATION

There are two ways of telling a reader what a character says: indirect speech and direct speech.

Indirect speech

This is also known as 'reported' speech, when you don't use the speakers' exact words but report what they said, e.g.

* *The Captain said that there would be extra rations for the men.*
* *The teacher threatened to give extra homework if their work did not improve.*
* *The doctor told me how she had saved his life.*

Direct speech

You can use the speaker's actual words inside speech marks (' ', or sometimes " ") but there is a bit more punctuation needed!

* The most common punctuation is a comma.
  E.g. *'We are going to have a wonderful time,' he announced.*
  Here the comma is used at the end of the spoken words INSIDE the speech marks.

* If the speaker continues speaking, you need another comma before the next spoken words.
  E.g. *'We are going to have a wonderful time,' he announced, 'and everyone will take part!'*

* If you start the sentence with the speaker and speech verb, the comma comes before the speech mark and the speech begins with a capital letter.
  E.g. *Flora said, 'You don't have to go.'*

* Full stops, exclamation marks and question marks must be placed inside the speech marks.
  E.g. *'I'm not going!' she yelled.*

* And finally – new speaker = new line.
  E.g. *'I'm not going!' she yelled.*
  'Why not?' asked Mr Parker.

Tips	★ Notice that when the speech verb comes in the middle of one continuous sentence, the second group of words inside speech marks do *not* need a capital letter to begin them.
	★ The speech verb or pronoun after the spoken word always begins with a lowercase letter, while a PROPER NOUN begins with a capital, e.g.
	• *'Rubbish,' she said.*
	• *'Rubbish!' answered Mary.*
	• *'Rubbish,' Mary cried.*
	★ If the spoken words end with an exclamation mark or with a question mark, you still use a lowercase letter after the speech mark.

Apostrophes

Take special care with apostrophes! They can change the meaning of a sentence when used badly.

There are only two reasons why you need an apostrophe:
- to show that something belongs to somebody (possession)
- to show that a letter or letters have been missed out (omission).

Possession

The boy's homework shows that the homework belongs to the boy.

Be careful with plural nouns (more than one).
The boy's boots means the boots belonging to one boy.
The boys' boots means the boots belonging to two or more boys.

Omission

Sometimes a letter (or part of a word) is missed out to make a shortened form.

This often occurs in direct speech so that it sounds natural.
Could not becomes *Couldn't*   *Was not* becomes *Wasn't*
Captain can become *Cap'n*

Tips	★ **It** – this is the really tricky one. Learn the rule and you won't make mistakes! ★ The apostrophe is ONLY EVER used when a letter is missed out (the shortened form). E.g. *It is a great adventure* becomes *It's a great adventure.* ★ The apostrophe is NEVER EVER used to show possession with it. ★ NEVER EVER use an apostrophe with plural nouns UNLESS it shows possession.

Practice question

Read the passage below. All the punctuation has been stolen, even all the capital letters and full stops! Your challenge is to put it back in. Read the passage carefully and out loud before you start and you will see how important punctuation is to readers.

the ship had been becalmed before but never for so long some of the men lay about the decks that baked in the heat others stayed below hoping for cooler air but the smell of so many men in a small space soon sent them on deck again was that a breath of wind asked the first mate hopefully perhaps it was said capn jake i think youre right all hand to the sails he cried his voice reaching all through the tiny ship men women and children went scurrying aloft

Tip
There are:

9 capital letters	7 full stops	5 commas
2 apostrophes	3 sets of speech marks	1 question mark
1 exclamation mark		

Check your answer against the punctuated passage on page 62.

Organisation

Remember, you need to organise your writing into paragraphs.

Once you have carefully planned your writing, you must organise your ideas in a way that helps the reader to follow your writing.

Level 4 writers need to include an opening/introduction, a middle and an ending. Usually the middle consists of TWO paragraphs.

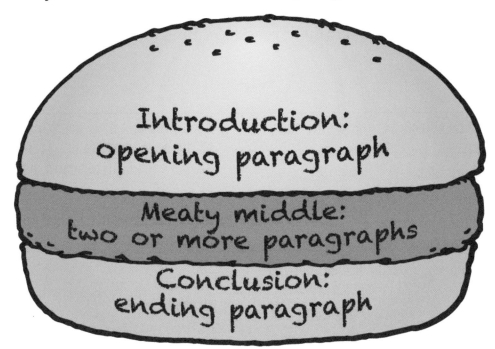

Fiction
Paragraphs usually signal that TIME is passing, or a new PERSON or a place has been introduced. Linking sentences are a good way to open new paragraphs. Here are some ideas:

Soon after   *Later on*
Without warning   *Just then*
This reminded her of the time...

Non-fiction
Paragraphs need to link your ideas together in an ARGUMENT, DISCUSSION, RECOUNT, REPORT, EXPLANATION AND LETTER WRITING. Linking sentences used to structure paragraphs in non-fiction could be:

First   *Then*
Next   *As a result of*
This means   *My strongest point is*
As I explained earlier *On the other hand*

Vocabulary

Think about the words you are going to use in your writing. If you choose them well they can improve the standard of your writing. They can give your reader a clear picture of what you mean and you will get your message across.

Remember, try to avoid repeating favourite words in a single piece of writing.

ADJECTIVES

Adjectives are used to describe a noun. They describe something or someone, e.g.
A red door.
A crying child.

Tips	★ Avoid using adjectives that say the same thing, e.g. *A frozen icy lake.* Instead, use two adjectives that say something different, e.g. *A vast icy lake.* ★ Avoid using adjectives in writing that you use when chatting, e.g. *really, very, nice, OK.* *We all ate a really nice meal* is dull. *We all ate a delicious meal* is better.	★ Adjectives that have the same initial sound as the noun work well in poetry and fiction. This is called alliteration, e.g. *The magical music.* ★ Remember, only use factual adjectives in non-fiction. Use them to add information, e.g. *The white football* rather than *the gloriously gleaming white football.*

Challenge 1

Change the adjectives in upper case to give readers a better picture in their mind's eye:

1. *This is a GOOD story.*
2. *The train had NICE purple doors.*
3. *After the race his face was VERY RED.*
4. *Mrs Lane is REALLY CROSS.*
5. *The tree had BIG flowers on its branches.*

Adverbs are used to describe a verb. They describe how something is said or done.

* *He gripped tightly.*
* *'I think so,' he answered quietly.*

Adverbs often end in 'ly'.

Challenge 2

Look again at the section on characters on page 26. In the extracts, can you find any adverbs that describe how characters speak or move?

Practice questions 1

Choose an adverb to make these sentences more interesting:

1 *He banged the book onto the table.*

2 *'You look out!' he whispered.*

3 *The monkeys climbed from branch to branch.*

4 *'It wasn't me!' she said.*

VERBS

Verbs tell us what someone or something is doing. Choose your verbs well and it can improve your writing. Which sentence do you think gives a better picture of what is happening?

Sunita put the shoe back into the box.
Sunita slammed the shoe back into the box.

Martin got his hat and raced to the door.
Martin grabbed his hat and raced to the door.

| Tip | ★ Avoid using *put* or *got*. They don't tell the reader much about what is happening. |

Practice questions 2

Choose a new verb to add interest to these sentences:

1 Hordes of menacing monkeys *swung* through the high treetops.

2 The proud princess *walked* along the streets of cheering crowds.

3 She *put* the china cups carefully in the basket.

4 The thief *got* through the broken attic window.

Spelling

The Spelling Test lasts for 10 minutes. You will be asked to spell 20 words from a passage that your teacher reads to you.

The test will cover:
- basic spelling rules
- more difficult or unusual words that might not fit basic spelling rules.

Below is a list of the 20 most frequently misspelled words in the National Tests over the last few years. Make sure you get them right this year!

change	*nastiest*	*technique*	*stripes*	*advertise*
designed	*swimming*	*perfectly*	*injured*	*regardless*
ready	*future*	*serious*	*attempts*	*vanishing*
produce	*surprise*	*individual*	*known*	*themselves*

The spelling rules that follow will help you. Read them through and make sure you understand them. Then remember to use them when you write.

Plurals

- Most words just add *s*: *road – roads; cup – cups; book – books; cat – cats*

- Some words need *es* to be added. Say them aloud and listen to how they sound. Words that end in a hissing or buzzing sound follow this rule. Words that end in *x, z, ch, sh* and *s* also follow this pattern:
box – boxes; bus – buses; watch – watches

- Words that end in *f* have a different pattern. You usually need to drop the *f* and add *ves*: *hoof – hooves; wolf – wolves*
But beware! There are exceptions. Try to learn these words:
gulf – gulfs; roof – roofs; dwarf – dwarfs/dwarves

- Words that end in *y* have a simple rule. If the letter before *y* is a vowel (*a e i o u*), just add *s*: *way – ways; toy – toys; monkey – monkeys*
If any other letter (a consonant) comes before the *y*, drop the *y* and add *ies*:
lady – ladies; spy – spies; story – stories

- Learn the irregular words: *mouse – mice; man – men; child – children*.
When you are reading, make a note of any irregular plurals you find and learn them.

Challenge

Look through books or dictionaries and find words ending in *y, x, z* and *s*. Change them into plurals.

Practice question

Change these words into plurals:

fox, road, bunch, wish, sound, life, tax, tree, drink, pirate, house, donkey, fly, bus

DOUBLING THE CONSONANT

Adding suffixes -er, -ed or -ing

There is a simple way to understand how to spell words that end in a consonant when you add -er, -ed or -ing. Listen to the sound the vowel makes.

Vowels can make short sounds or long sounds.
Stop has a short 'o' sound.   *Boat* has a long 'o' sound.

The rule is: double the consonant when the vowel is short.
Stop – stopping   *Boat – boating*

Challenge

1. Divide these words into two lists. Put all the words with short vowel sounds in one list, and all the words with the long vowel sounds in the other list.
    bin, line, paper, chat, choose, flutter, reign, wet, meet, light, float, dot

2. Look through some books and add four new words to each list.

3. Add the ending -er, -ed or -ing to the new words to make a different word.

4. Check the vowel sound to see which words need to have a double consonant.

5. Check your spelling in a dictionary.

Quick challenge

Tenses: Put these verbs into the past, present and future tenses. It is a good way to practise many of the spelling rules. If you find spelling some of them hard, look back at the spelling rules and learn them. If you still have trouble getting them right, read as much as you can and practise all you can.

Verb	Past tense	Present tense	Future tense
To fit	I fitted I have fitted I was fitting	I fit I am fitting	I will fit
To move			
To clap			
To keep			
To swim			
To fly			
To produce			
To try			
To pursue			

Reviewing your work

Rereading or reviewing your work is an important part of being a writer. No writer thinks their work is finished without rereading it and checking that it makes sense. Don't worry if you find things that need changing – there are always changes to be made. It is a good opportunity to look at ways in which your writing could be improved.

Here are some ideas to keep in mind when you are reviewing your work.

- **Make sure your reader will understand your main message.** For example, if you are writing a mystery story, will your reader want to find out what happens? Ask yourself if you have given too many clues to the ending. Is there a feeling of suspense and excitement? If you are writing an explanation, have you used connectives to help your reader follow the process that you are explaining? Would you be able to understand the explanation easily? If you are not sure, have another look at the guidelines for writing explanations.

- **Make sure you have followed the guidelines for the text type you are writing.** If you are not sure, go back and check. Keep the style constant and try not to slip from one type of writing to another. If you have started in the first person voice, have you kept to it all the way through your writing? Have you kept to the same verb tense? Don't get worried if you find mistakes – just correct them and try to remember for the future. No one gets it right all the time, but reviewing your work helps you to spot the errors that could lose you marks.

- **Check your spelling and grammar.** Look carefully as you read and, if a word doesn't look right, try it out a few times on a piece of paper. If you can, look it up in a dictionary and try to learn the correct spelling for the future. Read your sentences aloud. This will help you to hear when something doesn't sound right. When you think your grammar is not quite right, try saying the sentence in different ways and rewrite it a few times. Pick the one that you think sounds best and don't be afraid to make changes. Go back and check for any simple mistakes. Have you added all your capital letters and full stops?

Writer's tips	★ Read as often as you can. Reading helps you become familiar with good writing, helps you remember spelling patterns and helps you learn how to structure your sentences. Read as many kinds of books as you can. This will help you get ideas for your own writing.
	★ Keep a notebook and write down ideas, phrases, sentences and words that you like. If you read a phrase that might be useful, don't be afraid to make use of it. You can learn a lot from other writers' ideas. Jot them down in your writer's notebook. You never know when they might come in handy.

Writing and reading skills

Did you know that teachers are helping you develop your **writing** in at least eight ways? These are called 'assessment focuses' (AFs) and they are described here.

AF	Teacher language	This means...
1	Write imaginative, interesting and thoughtful texts	My writing is imaginative, interesting and thoughtful
2	Produce texts which are appropriate to the task, reader and purpose	I am able to write for different purposes and audiences according to the task set
3	Organise and present whole texts effectively, sequencing and structuring information, ideas and events	I can plan my writing and produce texts that sequence ideas, information and events within an appropriate structure
4	Construct paragraphs and use cohesion within and between paragraphs	I can use topic sentences and linking sentences to guide my reader through the text
5	Vary sentences for clarity, purpose and effect	I can use different types of sentences – simple, compound and complex – according to purpose and to create specific effects
6	Write with technical accuracy of syntax and punctuation in phrases, clauses and sentences	I am able to use different types of punctuation to make the meaning clear to my reader
7	Select appropriate and effective vocabulary	I can select and use a range of vocabulary, making choices according to purpose and audience
8	Use correct spelling	I can spell accurately

Reading is not just about being able to say and understand the words you see. Reading skills include the different ways you are expected to respond to a text. The seven assessment focuses for reading are:

AF	Teacher language	This means...
1	Use a range of strategies, including accurate decoding of text, to read for meaning	I can read for meaning
2	Understand, describe, select or retrieve information, events or ideas from texts and use quotations and references from texts	I can understand and pick out the appropriate quote, event or idea from a text and use PEE (Point, Evidence, Explain) to demonstrate my understanding
3	Deduce, infer or interpret information, events or ideas from texts	I can read and understand meaning that is only hinted at
4	Identify and comment on the structure and organisation of texts, including grammatical and presentational features at text level	I can identify the text type according to its presentational features and conventions. I can also comment on the writer's choice of text type to suit purpose
5	Explain and comment on the writer's use of language, including grammatical and literary features at word and sentence level	I can explain why the writer has made certain language choices (imperative verbs, emotive language, figurative language, formal/informal etc.)
6	Identify and comment on writers' purposes and viewpoints and the overall effect of a text on the reader	I can identify the writer's purpose and viewpoint and comment on how this affects the reader
7	Relate texts to their social, cultural and historical contexts and literary traditions	I can see how texts fit into their cultural and historical traditions

Reading comprehension

ABOUT THE READING TEST

The Reading Test comes in the form of two booklets – one containing the texts you will read and another with the questions and space for your answers.

You have one hour to read the booklets and answer all the questions.

Reading the texts

Read the text in the booklet. DON'T RUSH. Make sure you read the contents page; it has key information which prepares you for the types of texts you will be reading, for example *A country of colour* – a brief summary of how South Africa has changed in recent years.

DON'T RUSH!

If there are words you don't understand, read on and perhaps the paragraph will make sense anyway.

The questions

Always read the question carefully before you write. Look at the top of the page; it will tell you which section of the reading booklet you need to look at.

There are different types of questions which you will begin to recognise.

★ Some questions require a short answer, for example *who, what, when* style questions.

★ Some questions require a longer answer, for example *why, how, do you think* questions.

★ Some questions involve no writing at all, but instead you will need to circle the right answer, tick some boxes or match up ideas.

★ You might be asked to comment on why an author has used a particular word or phrase.

★ You could be asked about how a text is organised, for example pictures, subheadings, text in boxes, bold print, etc.

★ Some questions ask for your opinions and views – remember to link these to the text.

Answering the questions

After you have read the question, look across in the margin and you will see how many marks the question is worth (these usually range from 1 to 3 marks). This should help you to structure your answer. You must REFER TO THE TEXT in your answers – you can read the reading booklet as many times as you want! Although some of the questions require deep thinking, the answers will always relate to the reading booklet.

REFER TO THE TEXT

Reading between the lines

Authors don't always tell you exactly what is happening. They often give you clues to help you work it out for yourself.

> Josh cried long and deep into his hands. The lead hung from his pocket like a wilted flower and the hewed tennis ball was still wet from its last game with Spike. Had this actually happened? The smell of burnt tyres and the angry face of the driver told him it had.

1 What was hanging from Josh's pocket?

The answer can be found in the text itself – the lead.

2 What or who is Spike?

The text doesn't actually say, but from reading the clues (lead and chewed tennis ball) it becomes clear that Spike is a dog.

3 What has just happened?

Again, the text doesn't actually say, but you can draw your own conclusion from the text. 'The smell of burnt tyres', 'the angry face of the driver' and Josh's distress all imply that Spike has been hit by a car.

Top tips	★ Check how many marks each question is worth:
	  – One mark usually means the answer is in the WORDS of the text.
	  – Two or three marks usually mean that you are being asked to work out what the author meant – to read between the lines – or to draw on your own knowledge and experience.
	★ Always answer 2- or 3-mark questions with evidence or examples from the text.
	★ When a question begins *Why do you think …?* or *How do you know …?* you should always BACK UP YOUR ANSWER with examples from the text.

Achieving Level 4 reading

At Level 4, you show that you can understand a range of texts and understand their ideas, themes, events and characters. You show that you are beginning to use inference and deduction to read between the lines and can bring your own experiences into your understanding. You refer to the text when explaining your views. You can find and use ideas and information from different parts of a text.

If you can do all of these, you will achieve Level 4 and possibly even Level 5!

Text 1 (Non-fiction)

Go Ape!

The following text is taken from a leaflet to advertise an outdoor adventure park called *Go Ape!*

It's not in the dictionary, but if it was, Go Ape would be described as a 'high-wire forest adventure'.

That means we build giant obstacle courses up in the trees using ladders, walkways, bridges and tunnels made of wood, rope and super-strong wire, and top it all off with the country's best zip lines (including the longest at 426 metres – check it out on You Tube).

We then kit people out with harnesses and pulleys, give them a 30-minute safety briefing and training and let them loose into the forest, free to swing through the trees. Of course, instructors are always on hand, regularly patrolling the forests.

The result is spectacular. The Go Ape experience gets the adrenalin pumping, gets people out of their comfort zones and above all (no pun intended), it's just great fun.

How safe is it? When you're 40-feet up in the air and walking across a wire the thickness of one of your fingers, you need to know you're safe. We take safety extremely seriously and we ensure everyone who comes to Go Ape knows what they're doing and has the skills to complete a course without putting themselves or anyone else in danger. Before you head out onto the course, you'll be given a half-hour safety briefing by one of our qualified instructors. Here you'll learn and try out the obstacles at low levels, and get to grips with the equipment. It's not complicated, but it's important stuff and it will give you confidence to enjoy your time up in the trees.

Guidelines for participants:
Minimum age: 10 years
Minimum height: 1.4 m (4ft 7")
Maximum weight: 130 kg (20.5 stones)
Maximum number of participants: 14 per session

Tips	★ Read the text all the way through, then reread it more slowly. If you do not understand any of the vocabulary, read on through the sentence or the paragraph and see if that helps you to understand the word.
	★ When you have read it twice, think about the purpose of the text. Is it to entertain you, make you think in a certain way or give you facts and information?
	★ Read all the questions before you try to answer them. Check that you understand what each question is asking you to do.

Practice questions

If you need more space for your answers use extra paper.

(1) How tall do you have to be to take part in a 'Go Ape' visit?

_____

AF2

[ ] 1

1 mark

(2) This is an advert for *Go Ape*. Why do you think the designer chose to include photographs in the advert?

_____

AF4

[ ] 2

1 mark

(3) Find and copy a phrase which suggests *Go Ape* gives a real challenge to people who do not have much adventure in their lives.

_____

AF5

[ ] 3

1 mark

(4) Why is it important to try low obstacles first?

_____

AF3

[ ] 4

1 mark

(5) How long is the zip line at *Go Ape*?

_____

AF2

[ ] 5

2 marks

(6) Imagine you have been to *Go Ape*. Using the advert, write about your experience.

_____

_____

AF7

[ ] 6

2 marks

(7) List **three** ways in which *Go Ape* prepares you before you go on the high-wire forest adventure?

_____

_____

_____

AF3

[ ] 7

3 marks

(8) Tick **three** materials which the tunnels are made from.

Super-strong wire [ ]   Wood [ ]   Clay [ ]

Plastic [ ]   Rope [ ]   Glass [ ]

AF2

[ ] 8

3 marks

HOW DID YOU DO? See page 63 for the answers.

Total marks [ ]

Text 2 (Non-fiction)

Interview with Valerie Bloom

Where do you get your ideas from?

Ideas come from all over. Sometimes I read something, I listen to the radio, I watch television, I listen to people talking. I eavesdrop quite a lot I'm afraid. I get ideas from that. Sometimes they just jump up and hit you over the head when you're least expecting it, which is why, wherever I go, I have a notebook, because as soon as the ideas come, I jot them down.

Why do you write poetry?

I write poems because I like to be able to say a lot in a few words and you do that with poetry. I love playing around with words, which you can do with poetry, not so much with prose: I do write prose as well, I write novels. I enjoy doing that as well. But the other thing about writing poetry is that you can write a poem and have a finished product in a very short time, so I can write a poem in the bath, I can write a poem on the train, I can write a poem in my hotel room, so I can have a book finished in a short time.

Does music influence your writing?

Music is a big influence. I came from Jamaica. In the Caribbean, the art-forms are not separate. You don't just have poetry in one section and music in another, they are all inter-related. So you would get a poem which has singing and dancing and so on and I draw on that culture when I write. A lot of my poetry draws on folk songs quite a lot and I use rap in my writing and all those musical forms that I grew up with influence my writing.

What do you like doing when you're not writing?

I like cooking, I like gardening, especially working with my bonsai tree. I get very calm and peaceful feelings working with my bonsai tree. It's very good for writing. I like playing word games. Games like Scrabble, though nobody will play with me any more. They say I make up words, but I don't really.

Who do you think of when you're writing a poem?

Mainly I'm thinking about myself. I'm thinking about what excites me, what makes me laugh, what makes me sad or whatever. If I can write for myself and the number of people who are inside me, the child, or the old person, or the man, or the boy or the girl, then I think I will reach other people. Occasionally, when I'm writing poems for performance I think about the audience and I think what they would like to do and what I can give them to do so they can become part of the poem.

Tips	★ Read the text all the way through, then reread it more slowly. If you do not understand any of the vocabulary, read on through the sentence or the paragraph and see if that helps you understand the word.
	★ When you have read it twice, think about the purpose of the text. Is it to entertain you, make you think in a certain way or give you facts and information?
	★ Read all the questions before you try to answer them. Check that you understand what each question is asking you to do.

Practice questions

If you need more space for your answers use extra paper.

(1) Find and copy a phrase from the interview which explains why Valerie always takes a notebook with her wherever she goes.

_____

_____

AF3

[ ] 1

1 mark

(2) Tick the box which shows the country Valerie is from.

England [ ]   China [ ]   Jamaica [ ]   Spain [ ]

AF2

[ ] 2

1 mark

(3) Why is it difficult for Valerie to find people to play Scrabble with her?

_____

_____

AF2

[ ] 3

1 mark

(4) This interview has been published on a website. In what other format might it be published?

_____

AF7

[ ] 4

1 mark

(5) Valerie's words are written in the first person during this interview. Give another feature that shows this is an interview.

_____

_____

AF4

[ ] 5

1 mark

(6) Tick **two** boxes which show what Valerie's hobbies are.

Football [ ]   Playing the flute [ ]

Cooking [ ]   Singing [ ]

Gardening [ ]   Going to the cinema [ ]

AF3

[ ] 6

2 marks

HOW DID YOU DO? See page 63 for the answers.

Total marks [ ]

53

Text 3 (Fiction)

Bootleg

This extract has been taken from a book called *Bootleg* by Alex Shearer. It is set in the future when the government is forcing everyone to lead healthier lives.

Chocolate addicts Smudger and Huntly watch in horror as chocolate is banned from the shops and Chocolate Troopers arrest anyone caught with sweets. In this part of the story, it has been a long time since the boys have had chocolate and they go to try and buy some from a secret chocolate seller known as a bootlegger. They are kicking a bottle around as they wait for the chocolate seller.

After a few minutes, the man closed the bonnet of his van and sauntered over to where the boys were playing.

'Having a kickabout, lads?' he asked.

'That's it,' Smudger said. It was pretty obvious what they were doing.

'Hungry work kicking a ball about,' the man continued.

Huntly and Smudger exchanged a look. They stopped kicking the bottle.

'Yes,' the man went on, 'very hungry work is kicking a ball – or even a bottle – about. Makes you long for some kind of high-energy food supplement. Something full of energy to give you a bit of a *Boost*! Something with a bit of *Fruit and Nut* in it. Makes you wonder how they cope on the rest of the *Galaxy*. Makes you wonder if they play football on *Mars*. I sometimes wonder if there's life up there in the *Milky Way*. But you'd have to be quite a *Smartie* pants to know the answer to that one.'

And having delivered this odd speech, the man returned to his van and stood by the back door, leaning on the roof, and staring up at the sky. Huntly and Smudger looked questioningly at each other. Was this him? The black marketeer? He certainly didn't look like one. Not for a moment. He seemed quite ordinary. You'd never have thought –

But yes! That was the whole idea. You'd never have suspected for a moment.

Huntly and Smudger walked over towards the van, just as casually as the man had a few seconds earlier. At their approach he wordlessly reached out, turned a handle and opened the rear doors, so that the two boys could see inside.

'Take a look, lads,' he said. 'Shop around. Whatever you fancy.'

They looked into the van. Then they gawped, with eyes like saucers and expressions of such surprise that the chocolate seller almost laughed.

There was everything in there! Every chocolate bar you could name or think of. The van was full up with Dairy Milk, Twix, Rolos, the lot.

Practice questions

If you need more space for your answers use extra paper.

1 What are Smudger and Huntly playing football with?

_____

AF2

1

1 mark

2 When the bootlegger opens the van, the author describes Huntly and Smudger's reactions as 'Then they gawped, with eyes like saucers'. What does the writer's choice of words tell you about how the boys felt when they looked into the van?

_____

_____

AF4

2

1 mark

3 Why is the man leaning on the roof and staring up at the sky? Tick the right answer.

He is looking at the sun. ☐   He is very hot. ☐

He is fixing his van. ☐   He is waiting. ☐

AF3, 4

3

1 mark

4 The man says: 'Something with a bit of _Fruit and Nut_ in it. Makes you wonder how they cope on the rest of the _Galaxy_. Makes you wonder if they play football on _Mars_.'
Why have some of the words here been put in italics?

_____

_____

AF4

4

2 marks

5 Huntly and Smudger 'looked questioningly at each other' when deciding what to do as they looked at the chocolate seller. Why do you think they do this? Tick **two** answers below.

They are nervous and worried they may get caught. ☐

They are hot and tired in the sun. ☐

They are thinking about their homework. ☐

They are not sure if they can trust the chocolate seller. ☐

AF6

5

2 marks

HOW DID YOU DO? See page 63 for the answers.

Total marks ☐

Text 4 (Poetry)

Daddy fell into the pond

Alfred Noyes

Everyone grumbled. The sky was grey.
We had nothing to do and nothing to say.
We were nearing the end of a dismal day,
And then there seemed to be nothing beyond,
Then
Daddy fell into the pond!

And everyone's face grew merry and bright,
And Timothy danced for sheer delight.
'Give me the camera, quick, oh quick!
He's crawling out of the duckweed!' Click!

Then the gardener suddenly slapped his knee,
And doubled up, shaking silently,
And the ducks all quacked as if they were daft,
And it sounded as if the old drake laughed.
Oh, there wasn't a thing that didn't respond
When
Daddy fell into the pond!

Tips	★ Read the text all the way through, then reread it more slowly. If you do not understand any of the vocabulary, read on through the sentence or the paragraph and see if that helps you understand the word.
	★ When you have read it twice, think about the purpose of the text. Is it to entertain you, make you think in a certain way or give you facts and information?
	★ Read all the questions before you try to answer them. Check that you understand what each question is asking you to do.

Practice questions

If you need more space for your answers use extra paper.

1 What did Timothy do when Daddy fell into the pond?

_____

AF2

1

1 mark

2 *'Give me the camera, quick, oh quick!*
He's crawling out of the duckweed!' Click!

What is happening when 'click' comes at the end of this verse?

_____

AF6

2

1 mark

3 How is the atmosphere different in the final verse of the poem?

_____

_____

_____

AF3,5

3

2 marks

4 In the first verse, the author chooses to place the word 'Then' by itself. What is the effect of this?

_____

_____

_____

AF5

4

2 marks

5 Find and copy **three** words or phrases in the first verse which show that it was a really miserable day for everyone.

_____

_____

_____

AF5

5

3 marks

6 Why do you think the author included direct speech in the middle of this poem?

_____

_____

_____

AF6

6

2 marks

HOW DID YOU DO? See page 63 for the answers.

Total marks

57

Handwriting

Handwriting is teacher assessed as part of wider writing assessment. Do your best to always keep your handwriting neat and easy to read!

The golden rules

- Space out words and sentences evenly.
- Write on the lines if you are using lined paper.
- Use a pen or pencil you feel comfortable with and always use an eraser to rub out mistakes.
- Keep the letters the same size.
- Write so everyone can read your writing!

Example: 1

If your handwriting looks like this, you need to work on:
- joining up letters so they flow together neatly
- keeping the letters the same size
- spacing out the letters evenly. Some of these words are quite squashed!

Once upon a time, long ago there was a princess. She was the most beautiful princess in the world. Her dress sparkled as much as her charming attitude. She was the happiest prettiest person in the world.

Example: 2

If your handwriting looks like this, you need to work on:
- making sure all, not just some, of the letters are joined together
- getting the ascenders (the upward strokes like *d* and *b*) to lean in the same direction.

Once upon a time, long ago there was a princess. She was the most beautiful princess in all the land. Her dress sparkled as much as her charming attitude. She was the happiest, prettiest person in the world.

Overall, the shape and size of the letters are even and the writing is easy to read.

Example: 3

This is an example of excellent handwriting! The letters are all correctly formed and are evenly sized and spaced. The other good thing about this handwriting is that it has its own style, so try to develop a style of your own.

Once upon a time, long ago there was a princess. She was the most beautiful princess in all the land. Her dress sparkled as much as her charming attitude. She was the happiest, prettiest person in the world.

Hints and Tips	★ Compare a sample of your handwriting with the ones on this page. Which one is it most like? What are you doing well? What do you need to work on to make it better? ★ Go over what needs to improve with a highlighter pen, then rewrite the same sample, making as many improvements as you can. ★ Practise a few sentences at a time, rewriting them and making improvements. ★ Try especially hard to join the letters – it really speeds up writing!

Glossary

Adjectives words that add information or description to nouns

Adverbs words that add information or description to verbs

Cause what makes something happen

Character someone in a story; what someone is like, personality

Comprehension understanding

Conclusion the end of something; the resulting idea or thought about something

Connectives words that are used to link sentences and paragraphs

Deduction the use of evidence in the text to work out what the author is telling you, to read *between* the lines

Dialogue the words spoken by characters in a story

Effect the result of something happening

Emotive appealing to the emotions and making us feel in different ways

Evidence something that proves what you think or believe

Fiction stories that are imagined, not real

Imperative verbs that give a command, e.g. *Go* or *Put*

Inference the use of your own knowledge *and* the evidence in the text to come to a conclusion about what the author means, to read *beyond* the lines

Issue a matter or subject for discussion

Logical resulting naturally

Non-fiction texts that give you information

Omission missing out

Paragraphs a number of sentences grouped together, usually linked by idea, topic, time, place or theme

Passive voice a verb form where the action is done by someone else, e.g. *it was thrown*. The 'opposite' of this is the **active voice**, where the subject of the sentence does the action, e.g. *he threw it*

Possession owning

Problem something that goes wrong

Proper noun a noun that names a person, place or organisation

Recommendation what you think should be done

Resolution how a problem is sorted out

Review look back at critically or carefully

Setting where a story takes place

Stereotype a character, usually in a fairy story or traditional tale, who has no real distinguishing characteristics, e.g. *a bad witch, a handsome prince*

Summary a short piece of writing that sums up the main points

Theme an idea that a story or poem is about

Learning objectives for Primary English

This chart shows you the objectives required to achieve Level 4 in English.

Strand	Year 5	Year 6
Word structure and spelling	• Spell words with unstressed vowels (*doctor*, *around*) • Know and use prefixes and suffixes like *im-, -ir-, -cian* • Group and classify words by their spelling patterns and their meanings	• Spell familiar words correctly; use a range of strategies to spell difficult or unfamiliar words • Edit, proofread and correct spelling in your own work, on paper and on screen
Understand and interpret texts	• Make notes on and use evidence from across a text • Infer writers' perspectives • Compare different types of texts; identify their structure • Know that a word can mean different things in different contexts • Explore how writers use language to create comic and dramatic effects	• Quickly decide on a text's value, quality or usefulness • Understand a text's themes, causes and points of view • Understand how writers use different structures to create an impact • Explore how word meanings change when used in different contexts • Recognise rhetorical devices used to persuade and mislead
Engage with and respond to texts	• Reflect on reading habits and plan your own reading goals • Know different ways to explore the meaning of texts • Compare how a theme is presented in poetry, prose and other media	• Read widely; discuss your own reading with others • Read longer texts • Compare how writers from different times and places present experiences and use language
Create and shape texts	• Reflect on your own writing; edit and improve it • Experiment with different forms and styles when writing stories, non-fiction and poetry • Use direct and reported speech, action and selection of detail to vary pace and viewpoint • Create multi-layered texts, including use of hyperlinks and linked web pages	• Set yourself challenges to extend achievement in writing • Use different techniques to engage and entertain the reader in narrative and non-narrative • Select words and language, drawing on your knowledge of literary features • Integrate words, images and sounds imaginatively for different purposes
Text structure and organisation	• Experiment with the order of sections and paragraphs to achieve different effects • Change the order of material within a paragraph, moving the topic sentence	• Use varied structures to shape and organise text coherently • Use paragraphs to achieve pace and emphasis
Sentence structure and punctuation	• Adapt sentence construction to different text types and readers • Punctuate sentences accurately, including using speech marks and apostrophes	• Express meanings, including hypothesis, speculation and supposition, by constructing sentences in varied ways • Use punctuation to clarify meaning in complex sentences
Presentation	• Adapt handwriting for specific purposes • Make informed choices about which ICT program to use for different purposes	• Use appropriate handwriting styles for different purposes • Select from a wide range of ICT programs to present text effectively and communicate information and ideas

Answers

Page 10 – Recount: Challenge
First, Next, Then, After, Finally

Page 11 – Recount: Example answer 1
Monday: Went to audition for school play. It's called The Lost Boys. We all went to the hall after school but not many boys came – Miss Jenkins was a bit cross. We'd to stand at the front one at a time and read a poem that Miss Jenkins gave to us. My voice shook! Aargh! But I got the part of the Nanny, though really wanted to be Wendy. Carly got Wendy. She's such a show-off. First rehearsal is lunch time tomorrow. I haven't got lots of lines to learn so that is good. Can't wait because I'm going to be a famous actor when I grow up!

Page 13 – Instructions and procedures: Example answer 2

Getting dressed

What you need	What you do
Pants Socks T-shirt Trousers Sweatshirt Trainers	First put on the pants. These are small and white with three holes in them. Put your legs through the two smaller holes. Next put on the socks. There are two of these. They are long, grey tubes. Put one on each foot. Then put on the T-shirt. It goes over your head and has two holes for your arms. Put on the trousers. These are also grey but are much bigger than the socks. They go over the pants and socks. Now put on the sweatshirt over the T-shirt. It is blue and has a badge on the front. Finally put on the trainers. These are white and go on each foot. You will need to fasten the Velcro strips. Now you will look just like all the other pupils – apart from your green hair.

Page 14 – Non-chronological report: Challenge
(Sample answer) Introduction, Appearance, Food, Habitat, Breeding

Page 15 – Non-chronological report: Example answer 2
The Mintosaurus
Here you can see the newly discovered fossil of the Mintosaurus dinosaur.
This fossil was found by Sir Humbert Bumbert in South America in December 2008.
Amazing facts!
- *Length – 105 metres from nose to the tip of its tail.*
- *Height – 2 metres tall.*
- *Appearance – Mintosaurus had two short front legs and two powerful back legs. The front legs were short so it could bend down to graze. The back legs were strong to help it reach up to get leaves at the tops of trees. It had spines running down its back from the tip of its nose to the tip of its tail.*
- *Food – The Mintosaurus dinosaurs were herbivores. They ate the leaves of trees and also grazed on grass.*
- *Habitat – Mintosaurus has only been found in the jungles of South America.*
- *Did you know? The Mintosaurus dinosaur has been extinct for more than a million years!*

Page 17 – Explanation: Example answer 2
Dear Parents,
I am writing to tell you about a new type of lunch box that our class has invented. I hope it will make lunch times easier for your child.
The lunch box is made from recycled card, which means it is a greener box than the plastic ones most pupils use. It is split into four sections which open one after the other. This means your child will be able to eat the food in the right order. It also means that your child cannot just eat the bits they like!
There is one section for sandwiches. This opens first. When the sandwich section is empty, a spring goes off that opens the second section. This contains a drink. Next, the vegetable section opens. When the vegetable section is empty, the last section will open and your child can eat their fruit.
Using the new lunch box will help your child to eat a healthy meal at lunch time.
Yours sincerely,
Mr Andrews
Class 6A

Page 19 – Discussion: Example answer 2

Mobile phones should be allowed	Mobile phones should not be allowed
• Children can contact their friends • Parents can contact their children • Mobile phones are good fun • There are too many school rules already	• Children are already with their friends and don't need a phone to contact them • Parents can phone the school if they need to contact their children • They disrupt lessons • They cause jealousy about whose is the best phone

Page 20 – Persuasion: Challenge
have been offered, has been proven, should be eaten

Page 21 – Persuasion: Example answer 2
Football Stars Wanted!
Hill Street School Needs You!
Can you kick a football?
Can you run, tackle and dribble?
Do you want to learn how to play football?
Football is fun. You can make friends and keep fit too.

Hill Street School needs new players. Could you be one?
Try-outs
When – Thursday 12th September
Where – School playing field
Time – 3.30 p.m.
So Stop being a Couch Potato!
Come and be a Football Star!

Page 26 – Setting, characters and theme: Challenge 1

First extract: movement – strode; character – dangerous
Second extract: movement – stood straight and tall

Page 28 – Setting, characters and theme: Challenge 2

Lost and found

Beginning – Introduce one main character; establish setting
Build-up – Story gets going; character does something normal
Problem – Character finds or loses something or someone
Resolution – Lost thing/person is returned
Found thing/person not quite what it had seemed
Ending – Everything OK. Characters reflect on events

Wishing or wanting

Beginning – Introduce one main character; establish setting
Identify – What main character is wishing for or wanting
Build-up – Character goes in search of their wish
Problem – Character is stopped from getting what they want, often by another character
Resolution – Main character gets what he or she wanted
Ending – Character reflects on whether getting their wish was worth it

Page 29 – Dialogue: Challenge

1. surly, bad-tempered; 2. angry;
3. very worried, concerned or afraid;
4. frightened or angry

Page 35 – Grammar: Challenge 4

Simple sentence – He didn't look back.
Compound sentence – Halfway into his voyage home, he could contain himself no longer and he opened the locket.
Complex sentence – He set sail into the night, delighted with his daring exploits and laughing with excitement at the thought of the riches he knew would be his.

Page 36 – Grammar: Challenge

Hope put her coat as well as her scarf on. Next she put on her boots. Then her friends came round. Eventually they went to the park.

Page 38 – Grammar: Challenge

Mr Walsh was having an awful day. It was windy and wet so everybody was inside for lunch time. The children were behaving like wild animals and the classroom looked like a zoo.

Page 40 Punctuation: Practice question

The ship had been becalmed before but never for so long. Some of the men lay about the decks that baked in the heat. Others stayed below hoping for cooler air, but the smell of so many men in a small space soon sent them on deck again. 'Was that a breath of wind?' asked the first mate hopefully.
'Perhaps it was,' said Cap'n Jake, 'I think you're right. All hand to the sails!' he cried, his voice reaching all through the tiny ship. Men, women and children went scurrying aloft.
Give yourself an extra mark if you remembered to start a new speaker on a new line!

Page 42 – Vocabulary: Challenge 1

(Sample answers)
1. This is an *EXCITING* story.
2. The train had *VIVID* purple doors.
3. After the race his face was *COMPLETELY SCARLET*.
4. Mrs Lane is *LIVID*.
5. The tree had *ENORMOUS* flowers on its branches.

Page 42 – Vocabulary: Challenge 2

dangerously, angrily

Page 43 – Vocabulary: Practice questions 1

(Sample answers)
1. He *suddenly* banged the book onto the table.
2. 'You look out!' he whispered *menacingly*.
3. The monkeys climbed *rapidly* from branch to branch.
4. 'It wasn't me!' she said *firmly*.

Page 43 – Vocabulary: Practice questions 2

(Sample answers)
1. Hordes of menacing monkeys *clambered* through the high treetops.
2. The proud princess *strode* along the streets of cheering crowds.
3. She *placed* the china cups carefully in the basket.
4. The thief *scrambled* through the broken attic window.

Page 44 – Spelling: Practice question

fox**es**, road**s**, bunch**es**, wish**es**, sound**s**, li**ves**, tax**es**, tree**s**, drink**s**, pirate**s**, house**s**, donkey**s**, fl**ies**, bus**es**

Page 45 – Spelling: Challenge

Short vowel sound: bin, chat, flutter, wet, dot

Long vowel sound: line, paper, choose, reign, meet, light, float

Page 45 – Spelling: Quick challenge

Verb	Past tense	Present tense	Future tense
To fit	I fitted I have fitted I was fitting	I fit I am fitting	I will fit
To move	I moved I have moved I was moving	I move I am moving	I will move
To clap	I clapped I have clapped I was clapping	I clap I am clapping	I will clap
To keep	I kept I have kept I was keeping	I keep I am keeping	I will keep
To swim	I swam I have swum I was swimming	I swim I am swimming	I will swim
To fly	I flew I have flown I was flying	I fly I am flying	I will fly
To produce	I produced I have produced I was producing	I produce I am producing	I will produce
To try	I tried I have tried I was trying	I try I am trying	I will try
To pursue	I pursued I have pursued I was pursuing	I pursue I am pursuing	I will pursue

Page 51 – Text 1 (Non-fiction): Go Ape!
Practice questions

1. 1.4 m (4ft 7")
2. To persuade you to go, to let you see how it really is, to bring the experience to life.
3. Any one of the following:
   'The Go Ape experience gets the adrenalin pumping.'
   'Gets people out of their comfort zones.'
   'It's just great fun.'
4. It gives people confidence so they can enjoy their adventure in the trees.
5. 426 metres.
6. **Either** 1 mark for an expression such as 'Wow, amazing' and 1 mark for a reference to the tunnels, zip line, trees, ladders, walkways, bridges **or** 1 mark for an expression such as 'Arghhh, so scary' and 1 mark for a reference to the tunnels, zip line, trees, ladders, walkways, bridges.
7. A 30-minute safety training session, try out obstacles at low levels, try out/get used to the equipment.
8. Wood, rope and super-strong wire,
   3 correct = 3 marks, 2 correct = 2 marks and
   1 correct = 1 mark

Page 53 – Text 2 (Non-fiction): Interview with Valerie Bloom
Practice questions

1. 'Sometimes they just jump up and hit you over the head when you're least expecting it.'
2. Jamaica.
3. Because people say that she makes up words.
4. One of: newspaper, magazine.
5. Any one of: questions and answers, questions in bold, the questions and answers are given directly without using 'He said' or 'She replied' etc.
6. Cooking and gardening. *(1 mark for each)*

Page 55 – Text 3 (Fiction): Bootleg
Practice questions

1. A bottle.
2. The boys are amazed. Instead of saying 'the boys are amazed' the author says that their eyes were like saucers, meaning they opened them really wide with excitement.
3. He is waiting.
4. These are the names of chocolates and sweets. *(1 mark)* As he is a bootlegger/secret chocolate seller he doesn't want to say the word 'chocolate', so he is dropping hints/clues. *(1 mark)*
5. They are nervous and worried they may get caught. They are not sure if they can trust the chocolate seller.

Page 57 – Text 4 (Poetry): Daddy fell into the pond
Practice questions

1. He danced with sheer delight (and asked for the camera).
2. (Timothy) is taking a photograph/photo being taken.
3. The atmosphere changes because everybody comes alive and is happier. *(1 mark)* For example, the children and the gardener dance, the ducks quack and the old drake laughs. *(1 mark for an example of how the people change)*
4. Placing the word 'Then' by itself marks a change in the tone of the poem. *(1 mark)* It emphasises how exciting it was when Daddy fell in. The word 'Then' **introduces** that something exciting happened and it also **separates** the dull mood from the exciting mood. *(1 mark)*
5. Any three of the following:
   'Everyone grumbled.'
   'The sky was grey.'
   'We had nothing to do and nothing to say.'
   'We were nearing the end of a dismal day.'
   'And then there seemed to be nothing beyond,'
6. Direct speech adds to the excitement of the poem. *(1 mark)* It helps to bring the poem to life/helps you to imagine the scene. *(1 mark)*